COACHING AND COUNSELING:

A Practical Guide for Managers

Marianne Minor

CRISP PUBLICATIONS, INC.
Los Altos, California

COACHING AND COUNSELING:

A PRACTICAL GUIDE FOR MANAGERS

by Marianne Minor

CREDITS
Editor: **Michael G. Crisp**
Designer: **Carol Harris**
Typesetting: **Interface Studio**
Cover Design: **Carol Harris**
Artwork: **Ralph Mapson**

Copyright © 1989 by Crisp Publications, Inc.
Printed in the United States of America

English language Crisp books are distributed worldwide. Our major international distributors include:

CANADA: Reid Publishing, LTD., Box 7267, Oakville, Ontario Canada L6J 6L6. TEL: (416) 842-4428, FAX: (416) 842-9327

AUSTRALIA: Career Builders, P. O. Box 1051, Springwood, Brisbane, Queensland, Australia 4127. TEL: 841-1061, FAX: 841-1580

NEW ZEALAND: Career Builders, P. O. Box 571, Manurewa, Auckland, New Zealand. TEL: 266-5276, FAX: 266-4152

JAPAN: Phoenix Associates Co., Mizuho Bldg. 2-12-2, Kami Osaki, Shinagawa-Ku, Tokyo 141, Japan. TEL: 3-443-7231, FAX: 3-443-7640

Selected Crisp titles are also available in other languages. Contact International Rights Manager Tim Polk at (415) 949-4888 for more information.

Library of Congress Catalog Card Number 88-72253
Minor, Marianne
Coaching and Counseling: A Practical Guide For Managers
ISBN 0-931961-68-8

ABOUT THIS BOOK

COACHING AND COUNSELING: A PRACTICAL GUIDE FOR MANAGERS is not like most books. It stands out from other self-help books in an important way. It's not a book to read—it's a book to *use*. The unique "self-paced" format of this book and the many worksheets, encourage a reader to get involved and try some new ideas immediately.

This book introduces the basic concepts of *coaching and counseling* employees. It explains how these techniques differ and which skill should be used. Using the simple yet sound techniques presented can make a dramatic change in the overall success of your organization.

COACHING AND COUNSELING (and the other books listed in the back of this book) can be used effectively in a number of ways. Here are some possibilities:

—Individual Study. Because the book is self-instructional, all that is needed is a quiet place, some time and a pencil. By completing the activities and exercises, a reader should receive practical ideas on how to coach and counsel employees.

—Workshops and Seminars. The book is ideal for assigned reading *prior to* a workshop or seminar. With the basics in hand, the quality of the participation will improve, and more time can be spent on concept extensions and applications during the program. The book is also effective when it is distributed at the beginning of a session, and participants "work through" the contents.

—Remote Location Training. Books can be sent to those not able to attend "home office" training sessions.

There are several other possibilities that depend on the objectives, program or ideas of the user.

One thing for sure, even after it has been read, this book will be looked at—and thought about—again and again.

DEDICATION

This book is dedicated to my husband, Gregory C. Paraskou, who confirmed my uncertain suspicion that I could do whatever I set out to do. His belief in doing work that you love helped me take risks and build a thriving business that I love.

It is my hope that this book will help managers and supervisors learn to love *their* work by feeling more confident in the area of coaching and counseling.

Marianne Minor

PREFACE

This book is for anyone who wants to influence, direct, teach or motivate others, either formally as a manager or supervisor; or informally as a project leader, community advisor, a friend or parent.

Our lives provide us with numerous opportunities to demonstrate coaching and counseling skills. Anytime we *teach* someone a new skill, be it a child learning to walk or a project leader learning how to conduct meetings, we are coaching. Anytime a friend, coworker or family member seeks us out for *assistance or advice*, we are counseling.

Counseling and coaching are skills that can be learned through persistence and patience. If you have a sincere desire to develop and support others and the self-discipline to practice the specific strategies, you can become proficient in these areas.

The rewards from improving your counseling and coaching skills are many. *In your professional life*, you can use these skills to create optimal working conditions which include: proper orientation and training for employees, establishing clear responsibilities and standards, providing appropriate guidance and support during times of transition and insuring increased motivation and productivity through effective feedback. *In your personal life*, these skills will help you understand your friends and family members more deeply. In addition, you can use these skills to resolve personal conflicts. Your life can become more enriched and rewarding.

This book will enable you to analyze and develop your coaching and counseling skills. The emphasis will be on how these skills affect the workplace. However, the applicability of these skills to your personal life will be apparent. After you complete this book you will know practical guidelines and specific strategies to assist others in dealing with their personal problems and motivating employees to improve performance on the job.

CONTENTS

SECTION: I
THE WHAT AND WHY OF
COUNSELING AND COACHING

By the end of this section you should have a clear idea of what
counseling and coaching are and what skills they require. You will
also have a good idea of how effective you are as a counselor or
coach.

In order to get to this endpoint you will answer quizzes and
appraise your own skills.

But first let's start with the basics.

DEFINITIONS

Counseling: A supportive process by a manager to help an employee define and work through personal problems that affect job performance.

Coaching: A directive process by a manager to train and orient an employee to the realities of the workplace and to help the employee remove barriers to optimum work performance.

Counseling and coaching share many of the same skills. At times they may seem to overlap. When they do, remember the following diagrams. These diagrams (shown below) will help you differentiate the two processes.

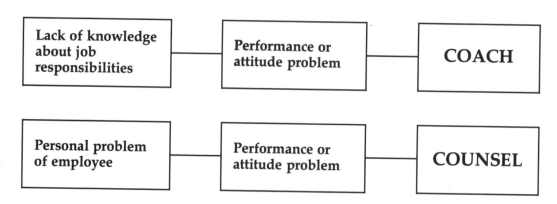

Lack of knowledge about job responsibilities	Performance or attitude problem	COACH
Personal problem of employee	Performance or attitude problem	COUNSEL

WHAT'S IN IT FOR ME?

Let's face it. Most of us need to see a personal payoff before we change our behavior. The same holds true for deciding to become the best possible coach or counselor you can.

THE BENEFITS OF COUNSELING

Why should you improve your counseling skills? Read each of the following statements below. Do you think they are true or false? Check your opinion and compare it with that of the author at the bottom of the page.

COUNSELING...

True *False*

☐ ☐ 1. Improves productivity of your business when employees feel listened to and supported.

☐ ☐ 2. Reduces turnover when employees feel they can vent their thoughts and feelings and deal with problems openly and constructively.

☐ ☐ 3. Makes your job easier by giving you warning of resistance or problems that may occur following changes.

☐ ☐ 4. Increases efficiency of your business when you understand the motives and needs of each employee and how he or she will react to organizational events.

☐ ☐ 5. Reduces conflict and preserves self-esteem when parties are really listened to.

☐ ☐ 6. Helps you solve problems before they occur.

☐ ☐ 7. Improves your decision-making when everyone's ideas are heard and employees' strengths and abilities are complemented.

☐ ☐ 8. Improves your career opportunities when you are known as a manager who can motivate employees and build constructive working relationships with bosses and peers.

☐ ☐ 9. Increases self-knowledge and personal satisfaction in your job.

☐ ☐ 10. Improves your self-confidence.

Answers: The author knows that all ten statements are true.
Did you agree?

THIS IS NEITHER COACHING
NOR COUNSELING

THE BENEFITS OF COACHING

Why should you improve your coaching skills? See if you agree with the author by deciding which statements are true and which are false. Compare your answers with those of the author at the bottom of the page.

COACHING...

True **False**

☐ ☐ 1. Makes your job easier when employees build their skill levels.

☐ ☐ 2. Enables greater delegation so you can have more time to truly manage versus ''do for.''

☐ ☐ 3. Builds your reputation as a people developer.

☐ ☐ 4. Increases productivity when employees know what the goals are and how to achieve them.

☐ ☐ 5. Develops sharing of leadership responsibilities.

☐ ☐ 6. Positive recognition and feedback increases employee motivation and initiative.

☐ ☐ 7. Increases likelihood of tasks being completed in a quality way.

☐ ☐ 8. Avoids surprises and defensiveness in performance appraisals.

☐ ☐ 9. Increases creativity and innovation of unit as employees feel safe to take risks.

☐ ☐ 10. Increases team cohesiveness due to clarified goals and roles.

Answers: If you thought all ten statements were true, then you agree with the author.

WHY MANAGERS AVOID COUNSELING

Assume you know the benefits of counseling but still avoid it. If this describes you, take heart you are not alone. Other managers gave the following reasons why they avoid counseling. Check any reasons that describe why *you* avoid it.

I avoid counseling because:

- ☐ 1. I don't have time.
- ☐ 2. Feelings are personal and not my business.
- ☐ 3. Counseling is for psychologists and psychiatrists.
- ☐ 4. Counseling feels awkward.
- ☐ 5. The employee won't listen to advice.
- ☐ 6. I think feelings about organizational changes are a waste of time and I just want to get the job done.
- ☐ 7. Feelings and concerns may go away.
- ☐ 8. I fear my own feelings.
- ☐ 9. I am afraid to give the wrong advice and be blamed for it.
- ☐ 10. Employee's career decisions are personal.
- ☐ 11. I fear uncovering frustration, complaints and dissatisfaction.
- ☐ 12. I feel responsible for solving the problems of the employee when I have enough problems of my own.
- ☐ 13. I lack self-confidence and know-how.
- ☐ 14. Employee may become dependent on me for empathy and advice.
- ☐ 15. Performance problems will resolve themselves.
- ☐ 16. I don't know how to explore or manage my own career let alone those of others.
- ☐ 17. I feel a loss of control when the employee cries or gets angry.
- ☐ 18. I don't have any solutions for the problems.
- ☐ 19. I overidentify with the employee's feelings or situations and can't be objective.
- ☐ 20. I don't have faith in the employee.

WHY MANAGERS AVOID COACHING

Do you find yourself avoiding coaching? Following are 20 typical reasons why managers avoid coaching. Check those that describe why *you* avoid coaching.

I avoid coaching because:

☐   1. I don't have time.

☐   2. Fear of failure.

☐   3. I don't want to scare or overwhelm a new employee.

☐   4. Coaching feels awkward.

☐   5. Nobody coached me; I have no role model.

☐   6. I have too many employees.

☐   7. I didn't set initial goals with employee.

☐   8. Employee won't listen.

☐   9. Employee should be able to figure things out on their own.

☐ 10. Employee will think something is seriously wrong.

☐ 11. Employee doesn't ask for help.

☐ 12. Performance is "almost" acceptable.

☐ 13. I will feel threatened.

☐ 14. Employee is motivated and doesn't need feedback.

☐ 15. Employee gets defensive.

☐ 16. Employee needs a certain period of learning time.

☐ 17. I get defensive.

☐ 18. My standards are obvious; employee should know what to do.

☐ 19. Nobody coached me.

☐ 20. I don't care whether the employee is developed.

CHARACTERISTICS OF EFFECTIVE COUNSELORS

Below are 20 characteristics employees have used to describe bosses who are effective counselors. Rate yourself in terms of what your employees would say about you. Be honest. We like to believe we do everything well, but unfortunately that's not always the case.

Scoring Key:

1 Seldom displayed;   **2** Sometimes displayed;   **3** Almost Always displayed

As a counselor, I:	Seldom	Sometimes	Almost Always
1. Treat employee's feelings as facts	1	2	3
2. Keep confidences	1	2	3
3. Facilitate discussions	1	2	3
4. Build employee's self-esteem	1	2	3
5. Reassure employee who is insecure	1	2	3
6. Support employee taking risks	1	2	3
7. Solicit employee's feelings, ideas and solutions	1	2	3
8. Let employee make own decisions	1	2	3
9. Care about employee	1	2	3
10. Am empathetic about employee's feelings	1	2	3
11. Help employee work out tough priorities	1	2	3
12. Am patient	1	2	3

	Seldom	Sometimes	Almost Always
13. Give full attention to discussion and am not distracted	1	2	3
14. Make employee feel confident about his/her ability to solve problems	1	2	3
15. Allow employee to vent dissatisfaction or concern with job	1	2	3
16. Consider employee's interests, skills and values when delegating work	1	2	3
17. Consider employee's goals when discussing career opportunities	1	2	3
18. Allow employee to grieve over a loss, personal or professional	1	2	3
19. Avoid acting like the expert on solving personal problems	1	2	3
20. Have sense of humor about organizational life	1	2	3
Total	____	____	____
Grand Total			

Scoring:

A total of **50–60** = Excellent; **40–49** = Fair to Good; **below 40** = need improvement

Now choose three characteristics that need the most improvement and write them below.

1. _____ 2. _____ 3. _____

The following page has an assessment for you to photocopy.* Give it to one or more of your employees who is capable of assessing your skills as a counselor.

EFFECTIVE COUNSELOR ASSESSMENT

_____   _____
        Date   Employee's Name

Thank you for taking the time to help me. I am interested in your honest feedback of my skills and attitudes. Don't feel you have to "fudge" and not tell the truth. To be the best manager, I need and want your candid responses.

Scoring Key:

1 Seldom displayed;   **2** Sometimes displayed;   **3** Almost Always displayed

As my boss, you:	Seldom	Sometimes	Almost Always
1. Treat my feelings as facts	1	2	3
2. Keep confidences	1	2	3
3. Facilitate discussions	1	2	3
4. Build my self-esteem	1	2	3
5. Reassure me when I feel insecure	1	2	3
6. Support me when I take risks	1	2	3
7. Solicit my feelings, ideas and solutions	1	2	3
8. Let me make my own decisions	1	2	3
9. Care about me	1	2	3

	Seldom	Sometimes	Almost Always
10. Are empathetic about my feelings	1	2	3
11. Help me work out tough priorities	1	2	3
12. Are patient	1	2	3
13. Give full attention to discussion	1	2	3
14. Make me feel confident in my ability to solve problems	1	2	3
15. Allow me to vent my dissatisfaction or concern with my job	1	2	3
16. Consider my interests, skills and values when delegating work to me	1	2	3
17. Consider my career goals when discussing career opportunities	1	2	3
18. Allow me to grieve over a loss, personal or professional	1	2	3
19. Avoid acting like the expert on solving personal problems	1	2	3
20. Have a sense of humor about organizational life	1	2	3

CHARACTERISTICS OF EFFECTIVE COACHES

Below are the 20 charactertistics employees have used to describe bosses who are effective coaches. Rate yourself in terms of what your employees would say about you. Be honest. Your answers are meant for you only.

Scoring Key:

1 Seldom displayed;   **2** Sometimes displayed;   **3** Almost Always displayed

---

As a coach, I:	Seldom	Sometimes	Almost Always
1. Capitalize on employee's strengths	1	2	3
2. Give employees visibility	1	2	3
3. Provide freedom to do job	1	2	3
4. Set standards of excellence	1	2	3
5. Orient employee to company values and business strategy	1	2	3
6. Hold employee accountable	1	2	3
7. Protect employee from undue stress	1	2	3
8. Encourage employee when he/she is discouraged or about to undertake new or difficult assignments	1	2	3
9. Provide information about the company and the employee's role in the attainment of company goals	1	2	3
10. Make performance expectations and priorities clear	1	2	3
11. Take time to build trust	1	2	3
12. Provide appropriate training and support when needed	1	2	3

	Seldom	Sometimes	Almost Always
13. Solicit and listen to ideas	1	2	3
14. View employees as partners and critical to the success of the unit	1	2	3
15. Serve as a good role model	1	2	3
16. Won't let employee give up	1	2	3
17. Don't divulge confidences	1	2	3
18. Explain reasons for decisions and procedures and give advance notice of changes whenever possible	1	2	3
19. Provide employees with regular feedback about their job performance	1	2	3
20. Give employees credit when they deserve it	1	2	3
Total	____	____	____
Grand Total	____	____	____

Scoring:

A total of **50–60** = Excellent; **40–49** = Fair to Good; **below 40** = need improvement

Now choose three characteristics that need the most improvement and write them below.

1. _____ 2. _____ 3. _____

The following page has an assessment for you to photocopy.* Give it to one or more of your employees who is capable of assessing your skills as a coach.

---

*Permission to photocopy for personal use only.

EFFECTIVE COACH ASSESSMENT

Date	Employee's Name

Thank you for taking the time to help me. I am interested in your honest feedback of my skills and attitudes as a coach. Don't feel you have to ''fudge'' and not tell the truth. To be the best manager, I need and want your candid responses.

Scoring Key:

1 Seldom displayed; **2** Sometimes displayed; **3** Almost Always displayed

As my boss, you:	Seldom	Sometimes	Almost Always
1. Capitalize on my strengths	1	2	3
2. Give me visibility	1	2	3
3. Provide freedom to do my job	1	2	3
4. Set standards of excellence	1	2	3
5. Orient me to company values and business strategy	1	2	3
6. Hold me accountable	1	2	3
7. Protect me from undue stress	1	2	3
8. Encourage me when I'm discouraged or about to undertake a new or difficult assignment	1	2	3
9. Provide information about the company and my role in the attainment of company goals	1	2	3

	Seldom	Sometimes	Almost Always
10. Make performance expectations and priorities clear	1	2	3
11. Take time to build trust	1	2	3
12. Provide appropriate training and support when needed	1	2	3
13. Solicit and listens to my ideas	1	2	3
14. View me as a partner who is critical to the success of the unit	1	2	3
15. Serve as a good role model	1	2	3
16. Won't let me give up	1	2	3
17. Don't divulge confidences	1	2	3
18. Explain reasons for decisions and procedures and give advance notice of changes whenever possible	1	2	3
19. Provide me with regular feedback about my job performance	1	2	3
20. Give me credit when I deserve it	1	2	3
Total	____	____	____

REVIEW SECTION I

You have now completed Section I. Can you recognize the differences between coaching and counseling? Do you have an understanding of when to use them?

If the answer is no, review the appropriate parts of Section I.

If the answer is yes, you are ready for Section II: When Should You Counsel or Coach.

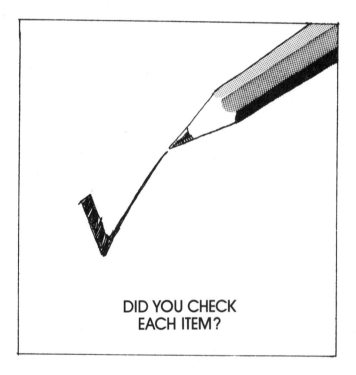

**DID YOU CHECK
EACH ITEM?**

SECTION: II
WHEN SHOULD YOU COUNSEL OR COACH?

Knowing when to counsel or coach is an important skill. It is the first step in the coaching or counseling process. When you can identify situations that need your expertise in a timely manner you are on your way to becoming an effective manager.

As you read through the following work situations, remember that they may not only apply to an employee reporting to you but to a peer, a boss or even to yourself.

A SUCCESSFUL COACH OR COUNSELOR LISTENS MORE THAN TALKS

WORK SITUATIONS THAT MAY REQUIRE COUNSELING

Check any that you have personally encountered:

- [ ] 1. Reorganizations
- [ ] 2. Layoffs—counseling for those who are laid off *and* those who are not
- [ ] 3. Demotions due to organization changes
- [ ] 4. Salary freezes; decreases in salary, status or responsibility
- [ ] 5. Employee faced with other career opportunities inside or outside of the organization
- [ ] 6. Employee faced with no career opportunities inside the organizaton
- [ ] 7. Employee unhappy with you as boss
- [ ] 8. Employee unhappy with work assignment
- [ ] 9. Employee who has conflict with peer
- [ ] 10. Employee that feels stressed or burned out
- [ ] 11. Employee who feels insecure about skills or ability to do the job
- [ ] 12. Employee quitting to take new job
- [ ] 13. Employee who has been promoted and is scared
- [ ] 14. Employee that shares personal problem requiring support
- [ ] 15. Employee whose personal problems are affecting performance of others
- [ ] 16. Performance problems that persist
- [ ] 17. Employee who is experiencing failure
- [ ] 18. Employee who is dissappointed in new job

Can you think of any other situations from your personal experience where counseling would have been effective?

19. _____

20. _____

WORK SITUATIONS THAT MAY REQUIRE COACHING

Check any that you have personally encountered:

- [ ] 1. Orientation and training of a new employee
- [ ] 2. Teaching a new job skill
- [ ] 3. Need to explain standards of the work unit
- [ ] 4. Need to explain cultural norms and political realities of the organization
- [ ] 5. Simple corrections to performance are required
- [ ] 6. Goals or business conditions change
- [ ] 7. You are new to a group
- [ ] 8. Employees facing new work experience
- [ ] 9. Employee that needs help setting priorities
- [ ] 10. Follow up to a training session
- [ ] 11. Employee that displays low or moderate performance
- [ ] 12. Employee who needs reinforcement for good performance
- [ ] 13. Employee wants to become a peak performer
- [ ] 14. Formal or informal performance reviews
- [ ] 15. Employee needs preparation to meet his/her future career goals
- [ ] 16. Employee needs preparation for more challenging work assignment
- [ ] 17. Employee needs self-confidence developed
- [ ] 18. When power or control battles are affecting team cohesiveness

---

Can you think of any other situations that may require coaching?

19. _____

20. _____

SIGNS OF PERFORMANCE AND ATTITUDE PROBLEMS

If an employee comes to you with a specific problem, great—your job as a manager has just been made easier. But how about those employees who never walk through your door even though you say your "door is always open." You may have to rely on your skill to recognize signs of performance or attitude problems.

Following are two lists of signs that can help you develop your managerial skills. Some will be obvious—others less so. You may have some signs of your own to add to the list.

SIGNS OF DECLINING PERFORMANCE	SIGNS OF POOR ATTITUDE
1. Decreased productivity	1. Little or no initiative
2. Poor quality work	2. Withdrawn
3. Missed due dates	3. Disinterested
4. Doing small task first	4. Increased complaining
5. Avoiding tougher jobs	5. Uncooperative
6. Disorganized	6. Blaming failure on others
7. Leaning on others for direction	7. Defensive
8. Away from desk for long periods	8. Avoids contact with others on team
9. Upward delegation	9. Lacking enthusiasm for job
10. Absenteeism	10. Irritability, depression
Add others:	Add others:

_____   _____

_____   _____

_____   _____

_____   _____

WHY EMPLOYEES DON'T GET THE JOB DONE!

CAUSES OF PERFORMANCE AND ATTITUDE PROBLEMS

Usually, there are three reasons people don't get the job done. Regardless of what reasons people may give, the answer may be one of these three:

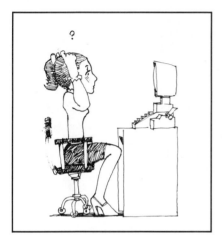

1. They don't know how.
- lack of instruction, orientation or training
- improper or lack of feedback

2. Something or someone keeps them from it.
- a physical or mental restriction
- not enough time
- wrong materials

3. They don't want to...
- previous good work unrecognized
- burn out
- unhappy with manager/job
- poor attitude

COUNSELING OR COACHING CHECKLIST

Before conducting either type of session, answer all of the questions below about the employee and the situation. Doing so will help you focus on whether you need to counsel or coach.

1. Does the employee know what is supposed to be done and when?

   yes ☐   no ☐

2. Have I defined the job description and skills required to do the job?

   yes ☐   no ☐

3. Does the employee have the skills required to do the job?

   yes ☐   no ☐

4. Has the employee been trained sufficiently in the organizational culture and skills needed to do the job?

   yes ☐   no ☐

5. Do I have the time it will take to sufficiently train and orient this person?

   yes ☐   no ☐

6. Have I adequately defined the ongoing job performance expectations for the employee?

   yes ☐   no ☐

7. If no, can anyone do the job? Is the standard realistic?

   yes ☐   no ☐

8. If no, can I revise the standards?

   yes ☐   no ☐

9. What is the specific difference between the present performance level and the desired performance level?

   _____

   _____

   _____

10. Is the difference important?

    yes ☐   no ☐

COUNSELING OR COACHING CHECKLIST (Continued)

11. Define the impact the performance problem has on . . .

    You: _____

    Employee: _____

    The unit: _____

    The team:_____

    The organization: _____

12. Does the employee want the job?

    yes ☐   no ☐

13. Does the employee have adequate resources to do the job?

    yes ☐   no ☐

    If no, what specifically does the employee need?

    _____

14. Are obstacles beyond the employee's control affecting performance?

    yes ☐   no ☐

    If yes, what specific obstacles?

    _____

    Can these obstacles be removed?

    yes ☐   no ☐

    If yes, what does the employee need from me during this time to help meet minimal performance standards?

    _____

15. Are consequences positive for positive performance?

    yes ☐   no ☐

16. Have I been giving high-quality feedback?

    yes ☐   no ☐

    If no, how can I improve?

    _____

    _____

COUNSELING OR COACHING
CHECKLIST (Continued)

17. Have I given immediate reinforcement for improvements?

    yes ☐   no ☐

18. Have I been inadvertently rewarding poor performance by ignoring it rather than coaching to correct it?

    yes ☐   no ☐

19. Does the employee trust me and feel I am here to help him/her be successful in this job?

    yes ☐   no ☐

    If no, what specifically can I do to build the trust?

    _____

    _____

    _____

    _____

20. Do I have a plan to develop the employee's skill or motivation?

    yes ☐   no ☐

    If yes, describe the plan in detail below:

    _____

    _____

    _____

    _____

    If no, develop a plan before conducting a session. Then, during your session, be sure you solicit the employee's ideas *first* before adding your own. Seriously consider the employee's ideas, and try to develop a plan that blends your ideas with his or hers.

FIVE CASE STUDIES TO EVALUATE YOUR SKILLS

Each of the five cases below describe typical situations a manager or supervisor can encounter on the job. Please specify what you feel is required: counseling, coaching, or both. Compare your answers with those of the author on the following page.

1. You have just hired Miguel who has a degree in Engineering. He has lots of energy and enthusiasm for his new job and is a project leader. You want to get him off on the right start.

   Counsel ☐ **Coach** ☐

2. Sally has been with your unit for one year now. She has just been promoted to Marketing Manager. She has shown creativity in her marketing campaigns and lots of drive. She has extremely high standards of performance, and pushes herself and others equally hard. Unfortunately, her behavior seems to have created a morale problem in her unit. She has her unit working overtime and weekends as she attempts to oversee every detail. Sally demands perfection. You have had several complaints from her employees.

   Counsel ☐ **Coach** ☐

3. Susan, Supervisor of Facilities, has been working for you for three years. She has been a superstar, increasing productivity in her unit by more than 70 percent in the last year. Due to her tremendous talents in managing people you have offered her a promotion to Manager of Facilities. She has stopped by your office to talk about her fears and insecurities regarding the new position. You have no doubt that she can do it well.

   Counsel ☐ **Coach** ☐

4. Wei-Ling is a production operator who has been a conscientious employee with a good track record. She shows a lot of initiative and enthusiasm for her job. She has stopped by your office to discuss a personal problem that may interfere with her job—she has just discovered that her mother is dying of cancer. She is very close to her mother and seems very upset.

   Counsel ☐ **Coach** ☐

5. Joe, one of your QC inspectors, has been with your group for six months. His performance has been substandard in many ways. He shows up late for work at least two days a week, is disruptive in departmental meetings and has let many defective parts pass through his station.

   Counsel ☐ **Coach** ☐

ANSWERS TO CASE STUDIES

1. **COACH** Miguel is a newcomer and needs direction, orientation and probably training.

2. **COACH** Sally needs direction and training on how to be a manager, i.e. setting realistic goals and using recognition to motivate employees. If after your coaching she continues to drive her unit hard, you may need to *counsel* her.

3. **COUNSEL** Susan is seeking you out to discuss her feelings. Her skills are not deficient

4. **COUNSEL** Wei-Ling has initiated discussion about a personal problem that may affect her work.

5. **COACH** Joe needs to understand the job standards and the importance of being on time, as well as the consequences of his performance. If his problems persist after your coaching session, he may require counseling.

How did you do? If your answers agreed with those of the author, then you are ready to go on to Section III. If you didn't agree with the answers, review the appropriate parts of Section II.

SECTION: III
HOW CAN YOU GIVE
EFFECTIVE FEEDBACK?

You should now know what coaching and counseling involve and when you should use each. Now you are ready to learn the most important skill to becoming an effective coach or counselor—namely how to provide honest feedback.

Whether you recognize it or not, you are constantly providing feedback. How you provide that feedback will often spell the difference between success or failure.

FOUR TYPES OF FEEDBACK

TYPE 1	DEFINITION	PURPOSE	IMPACT
SILENCE	No response provided. Example: "Silence."	Maintain status quo	• Decreases confidence (long term) • Reduces performance (long term) • Creates surprises during performance appraisals • Can create paranoia

TYPE 2	DEFINITION	PURPOSE	IMPACT
CRITICISM (negative)	Identifies behaviors or results that *were* undesirable, not up to standard. Example: "You did a poor job running that meeting this morning."	Stop undesirable behavior/results	• Generates excuses and blaming of others • Tends to eliminate other related behaviors • Decreases confidence • Leads to escape and avoidance • Hurts relationship

TYPES OF FEEDBACK (Continued)

TYPE 3	DEFINITION	PURPOSE	IMPACT
ADVICE	Identifies behaviors or results that are highly regarded and often specifies how to incorporate them in the future. Example: ''Remember to talk to Sue and include her ideas in the final report, so the report is comprehensive and up to date.''	Shape or change behavior/results to increase performance	• Improves confidence • Can improve relationship • Increase performance

TYPE 4	DEFINITION	PURPOSE	IMPACT
REINFORCEMENT (positive)	Identifies behavior or results that *were* desired; up to or exceeding standards. Example: ''The format of this report will make my job a lot easier. Thank you for taking the time to structure it this way.''	Increase desired performance/results	• Increases confidence • Increases performance • Increases motivation

HOW DO YOU USE FEEDBACK?

Think about the type of feedback you use in managing your employees. Then take the following quiz.

When I manage, I use this type of feedback:	Almost Always	Frequently	Occasionally	Never
1. Silence	☐	☐	☐	☐
2. Criticism (Negative)	☐	☐	☐	☐
3. Reinforcement (Positive)	☐	☐	☐	☐
4. Advice	☐	☐	☐	☐

WHAT KIND OF FEEDBACK DO YOU USE?

FEEDBACK MEMORIES: PAINFUL AND PLEASANT

Many times throughout our lives we receive feedback. Sometimes it is given directly, sometimes indirectly. Sometimes the feedback is positive, sometimes negative. If we are fortunate, the feedback helps us learn something about ourselves. But sometimes feedback creates negative feelings and does little to improve our performance.

Think about an "unforgettable negative feedback experience"...where the feedback given created negative feelings in you and answer the following statements:

1. Describe what it was about the way the feedback was given that created such a negative effect.

2. Was the feedback solicited or imposed?

3. What impact did this feedback have on your feelings and subsequent performance?

Now try to remember a time when you received positive feedback that increased your self-esteem and motivation and respond in the space provided:

1. Describe what it was about the way the feedback was given that created such a positive effect.

2. Was the feedback solicited or imposed?

3. What impact did this feedback have on your feelings and subsequent performance?

HOW TO GIVE EFFECTIVE FEEDBACK

1. **Make your feedback specific as related to behavior.**

   Good: "Henry, you have been 15 minutes late for the last three mornings, please explain why."

   Bad: "Henry, you are lazy and have a poor attitude towards your job."

2. **Consider your timing, either before the event in the form of advice, or immediately after it as positive feedback.**

   Good: (advice) "Sally, I'd like to review the content of your presentation with you before your speech next week so you can really do a 'good' job in front of the group."

   Bad: (criticism) "Sally, because you've done such a poor job in the past, I need to preview the speech you plan on giving next week."

   Good: (positive) "Sally, you did an outstanding job in organizing your presentation for the meeting. The speech was well-researched and logical."

   Bad: (positive but not specific) "Sally, good speech last week. Keep up the good work!"

3. **Consider the needs of the person receiving the feedback as well as your own. Ask yourself what he or she will get out of the information. Are you "dumping" or genuinely attempting to improve performance or the relationship?**

   Good: "Sue, I know how important it is to you to get the newsletter just right, and recognize you're under a lot of pressure right now. I will help you edit it this time, but I want you to take that editing class so you can handle it solo in the future."

   Bad: "Sue, you always need help with the newsletter. It's not my responsibility. Don't you think it's about time you learned how to edit the newsletter?"

4. **Focus on behavior the receiver can do something about.**

   Good: "Sam, we would appreciate you keeping the team informed about the status of the project?"

   Bad: "Sam, why are you are so introverted that you don't like to talk to other people?"

5. **Solicit feedback rather than impose it.**

   Good: "Linda, did you say you would like to learn how to handle your most difficult customer more effectively? Here are some things that have worked for me..."

   Bad: "Linda, I saw the way you handled Mrs. Dawson during this crisis. It really stinks."

HOW TO GIVE EFFECTIVE FEEDBACK
(Continued)

6. **Avoid labels and judgements by describing rather than evaluating behavior.**

   Good: "Steve, I have given you five chances to attend training programs in the last year and you haven't enrolled yet. Is there a problem?"

   Bad: "Steve, you are very lazy about improving your skills and don't seem to care about your career here."

7. **Define the impact on you, the unit, the team and the company.**

   Good: "Sarah, when you don't get your report to me on time, I can't get my report to my boss on time. This slows up decisions about resources needed for next month."

   Bad: "Sarah, can't you ever get your reports to me on time?"

8. **Use "I" statements as opposed to "you" statements to reduce defensiveness.**

   Good: "Tim, when you play your radio in the work area I lose my concentration. Would you mind turning it off during regular work hours?"

   Bad: "Tim, you are so inconsiderate of other people when you leave your radio on."

9. **Check to be sure clear communication has occurred.**

   Good: "Mary, do you know the importance of recording all my phone messages. Can you explain it to me so I know you understand?"

   Bad: "Mary, I'm sure you got it all, huh?"

10. **Give the feedback in a calm, unemotional language, tone and body language.**

    Good: "Joe, I'm sure your progress will be much faster now that you are clear on how to use this new machinery."

    Bad: "Joe, isn't it about time you improved your production with this machine!"

ADDITIONAL POINTS TO REMEMBER

1. Reinforcement is the most effective form of feedback.

2. Criticism is the most ineffective form of feedback.

3. The difference between criticism and advice is a difference in *timing*. Most criticism can be given as advice.

4. When feedback is mixed the impact is diluted. The employee ends up confused and not knowing what to do.

5. Criticism overpowers all other feedback.

6. Silence is not always "golden." It can be interpreted in a variety of ways.

POSITIVE FEEDBACK COMES IN MANY FORMS

KINDS OF REINFORCEMENT

In addition to one-on-one verbal reinforcement, employees may be motivated by other types of reinforcers. The best way to find out which are meaningful is to ask your employees directly and listen to them. Listen for values, interests and hobbies.

Here are 18 examples of reinforcers:

1. Being given control over job
2. Winning special projects
3. Having greater visibility to upper management
4. Being involved to a greater scope/depth
5. Having a choice in overtime
6. Having a choice in flex-time, schedule or vacations
7. Being offered the ability to travel
8. Receiving flowers
9. Receiving money
10. Receiving awards such as a plaque.
11. Having praiseworthy letters in file
12. Being given greater exposure to different parts of the organization
13. Receiving public praise
14. Receiving business cards or stationary
15. Having an improved office environment—new desk, window, office, etc.
16. Being given a dinner with spouse
17. Having the ability to attend classes and conferences
18. Being asked to observe customer visits

What additional reinforcers might motivate your employees?

_____   _____

_____   _____

_____   _____

WHAT BEHAVIOR DO I REWARD, IGNORE OR PUNISH?

It is crucial for managers to examine how they communicate what is desired or undesired performance and behavior. Take a few moments to write down the behaviors you reward in your unit, behaviors you ignore and behaviors you punish. Think in terms of who gets the best assignments, opportunities, public praise, exposure and benefits.

Behaviors I reward	Behaviors I ignore	Behaviors I punish

How should this be changed?

EACH OFFICE REFLECTS DIFFERENT INDIVIDUAL BEHAVIORS

CASE STUDIES ON GIVING FEEDBACK

WHAT TYPE OF FEEDBACK SHOULD THE MANAGER USE?

Write in the spaces provided the type of feedback you would use and what you would say in each of the following situations. Compare your answers with those of the author on the following page.

> **A** = Advice   **P** = Positive Feedback   **N** = Negative (criticism)   **S** = Silence

1. Fred, a recently hired marketing specialist, has just turned in his first monthly marketing report. Your impression is that the report was done in a hurry and was not well thought out. You did not train Fred in how to develop the report.
   You would use _____
   What would you say to Fred?

   _____

   _____

   _____

2. Carla has been in charge of materials distribution for the last 12 months. Recently you have received complaints from the production line supervisor that materials have been arriving late at the line.
   You would use _____
   What would you say to Carla?

   _____

   _____

   _____

3. Paula is your new secretary. She has just given you some letters you asked her to type. They were neat and error-free, and finished on time.
   You would use _____
   What would you say to Paula?

   _____

   _____

   _____

4. Don has just submitted his part of a proposal you are responsible for coordinating. It is Monday and you know he worked most of the weekend to get his piece to you. His deadline was pretty tight and you are grateful he put in the extra time to meet it. Unfortunately, you are racing-out the door to catch a plane with the proposal in your hand.
   You would use _____
   What would you say to Don?

   _____

   _____

   _____

ANSWERS TO CASES ON PAGE 37.

1. **ADVICE:** ''Fred, let's discuss how I would like to have your reports formatted as well as the content I need in the report. I want you to know who gets the reports and how they are used so you will know why they need to be done in this specific way. You are new and I want you to get off to a good start with these reports.

2. **ADVICE:** ''Carla, I'd like to discuss a concern I have with your materials arrival times. Let's discuss what happens when the materials are not on time and the effect it has on other people and departments. Can you let me know what interferes with you getting the materials on time? What can you do about it?''

3. **POSITIVE FEEDBACK:** ''Paula, I sure appreciate how well done these letters are! They are neat, have no errors, and were returned to me on time. Thank you.''

4. **POSITIVE FEEDBACK:** Send Don a card from the airport or hotel as soon as possible letting him know how much you appreciated him working hard like that and helping you out.

ACTION PLAN FOR GIVING FEEDBACK

Now that you know how important it is to give high-quality feedback, examine the feedback needs of your employees. Analyze who needs what kind of feedback and set a date for a feedback discussion.

Employee	Feedback needs	Date to discuss feedback
1. _____	_____ _____ _____	_____
2. _____	_____ _____ _____	_____
3. _____	_____ _____ _____	_____
4. _____	_____ _____ _____	_____
5. _____	_____ _____ _____	_____

FEEDBACK ACTION PLAN (Continued)

Now that you know how important feedback can be to your employees, think about yourself.

• How do you receive unsolicited feedback?

_____

_____

_____

• Do you solicit feedback from your employees, peers or boss on how you can help them?

_____

_____

_____

> Remember that a manager's ability to receive and solicit feedback can be just as important to his or her success as giving it.

SECTION: IV
HOW TO PLAN AND CONDUCT EFFECTIVE COUNSELING AND COACHING SESSIONS

Preparing For A Counseling or Coaching Session

When a counseling or coaching session goes poorly, it is usually because the manager has not prepared properly. At this point you should have answered the *Counseling/Coaching Questionnaire* included in Section II and know which type of session you need to conduct. You have already analyzed whether you are dealing with a performance problem or a personal problem.

Now you are ready to prepare for the session on the following page by doing each of the nine items that follow. Put a check mark next to each completed item.

PREPARING FOR A COUNSELING OR COACHING SESSION (Continued)

For my next counseling/coaching session I will prepare by completing each of the following steps. Place a ☑.

☐ 1. Consider how many sessions I will need, the degree of trust, and the employee's confidence level.

☐ 2. Be clear about my reason for the session and define my goals.

☐ 3. Review the work goals and past performance of the employee.

☐ 4. Give the employee notice of the time and place.

☐ 5. Allot a minimum of 30 minutes for the session.

☐ 6. Remove all distractions (phone, visitors, etc.) from the meeting place.

☐ 7. Remove physical barriers between myself and the employee (e.g. don't sit behind a desk).

☐ 8. Write out what I plan to say and rehearse it. Keep my notes in front of me during the session to avoid the feeling of losing control.

☐ 9. Plan to take notes to document the session, and develop a record of the corrective action plans and performance improvements.

COUNSELING PITFALLS TO AVOID

Following are some pitfalls if managers do not prepare properly. Check those pitfalls that you have experienced or observed.

☐   1. Manager has preconceived notions about what the real problem is.

☐   2. Manager has opinions about employee's choices and judges employee's decisions according to the manager's own values.

☐   3. Manager tells employee what he/she should or ought to do.

☐   4. Manager plays psychiatrist and attempts to diagnose or "treat" employee.

☐   5. Manager downplays employee's problem or pain by using clichés such as "cheer up."

☐   6. Manager moves into problem-solving mode from start, rather than listening.

☐   7. Manager does not empathize with employee's problems or feelings.

☐   8. Manager shifts focus to his/her problems or feelings.

☐   9. Manager over-empathizes with employee's problem or feelings.

☐ 10. Manager "rescues" employee by taking responsibility for decision making away from the employee.

☐ 11. Manager does not check with Human Resources or Personnel for assistance in problem beyond the manager's scope.

☐ 12. Manager has not investigated company resources such as employee assistance programs to assist in determining the real problem.

Write below any additional pitfalls you need to watch for that are not listed above.

_____

_____

_____

_____

COACHING PITFALLS TO AVOID

Read the following pitfalls managers can fall into if they do not prepare properly. Check those pitfalls that you have experienced.

☐   1. Manager can't determine real problem.

☐   2. Manager is unclear about what is expected.

☐   3. Manager doesn't have enough information.

☐   4. Manager exhibits bias towards employee or problem.

☐   5. Manager is inflexible.

☐   6. Manager loses control due to employee's hostile reaction.

☐   7. Manager becomes defensive.

☐   8. Manager doesn't solicit employee's suggestions or solutions.

☐   9. Manager doesn't listen to employee's story.

☐ 10. Manager fails to document evolving performance problems.

☐ 11. Manager fails to hold employee accountable in follow-up meeting.

☐ 12. Manager fails to reinforce improved performance.

Write below any additional pitfalls you need to watch for that are not listed above.

_____

_____

_____

_____

_____

GUIDELINES FOR CONDUCTING A SUCCESSFUL COUNSELING SESSION

You are ready to begin a counseling session. You feel confident. You have completed the preparation detailed at the beginning of this section. You have reviewed the counseling pitfalls and know to avoid them. Someone will answer your phone. You are ready to listen. Your notes and pencil are in front of you. Your employee walks in. You begin the session.

1. You put the employee at ease by being warm and friendly and using positive body language, lots of eye contact and physically facing the person.

2. You define the reason for the discussion if you called the session, or encourage the employee to define its purpose.

3. You avoid judgmental words like *should, must* or *ought*.

4. You ask open-ended questions about the employee's feelings and thoughts.

5. You paraphrase the content and feelings of the employee's message.

6. You summarize key points at the end of a discussion to clarify and seek understanding.

7. You encourage the employee to identify alternatives to solve the problem or resolve the issue.

8. You seek the employee's feelings and possible consequences of each of the alternatives.

9. You avoid expressing your views but remain alert to provide information on company policies that may help the employee make a decision.

10. You demonstrate empathy for the employee and show confidence in his/her ability to solve problems.

11. You provide support and/or resources when appropriate.

12. You refer to the employee to Personnel and/or an employee assistance program if the problem is beyond your scope.

13. You schedule a follow-up meeting to check on progress with employee.

The employee leaves. You sigh, then pat yourself on the back. You've completed a successful counseling session! Congratulations!

GUIDELINES FOR CONDUCTING A SUCCESSFUL COACHING SESSION

You are ready to begin a coaching session. You feel confident. You have completed the preparation detailed at the beginning of this section. You have reviewed the coaching pitfalls and know you can avoid them. Someone will answer your phone. You are ready to listen. Your notes and pencil are in front of you. Your employee walks in. You begin the session.

1. You put the employee at ease by being warm and friendly.

2. You define the reason for the discussion.

3. You express your concern about the area of performance you feel needs to be improved.

4. You describe the performance problem or area that needs improvement and define its impact on you, the employee, the unit, and the company.

5. You acknowledge and listen to employee's feelings.

6. You seek the employee's opinion on ways to improve performance.

7. You ask open-ended questions to encourage employee's analysis and draw out specific suggestions.

8. You let the employee know that you respect his/her ability to solve problems and develop solutions.

9. You offer suggestions when appropriate, but build on employee's ideas when possible.

10. You agree upon appropriate actions.

11. You schedule a follow-up meeting to ensure accountability and provide feedback on progress (within ten days.)

12. You promise to provide feedback on progress.

The session is over. You are relieved and pleased that it went so well. Congratulations!

WHAT TO DO WHEN ALL ELSE FAILS

Occasionally, despite coaching or counseling sessions, an employee's performance may continue to deteriorate or remain below acceptable standards.

When this happens, you as manager, must take responsibility for remedying the situation by choosing among the alternatives below. Before determining the best alternative, answer the questions next to each alternative.

Alternatives	Questions To Ask Yourself First
Restructure existing job	1. Does the employee possess enough strength in key areas of the restructured job? 2. Can tasks be eliminated or delegated where employee's performance is below standard?

Transfer to another job within the company	1. Can the employee make a contribution elsewhere in the company?
	
	2. Will a replacement requisition be cut if this person is transferred or terminated, or will I be left with no one to do the job?
	  a. Does the employee have the required intellectual and interpersonal capabilities?
	  b. Is the employee motivated to learn a new job?
	  c. Am I being realistic or simply avoiding responsibility for termination by transferring a "problem" employee to another area?

Disciplinary action and termination	1. Have I given the employee every chance to succeed?
	  a. Has the employee had adequate resources to do the job?
	  b. Has the employee been sufficiently trained and oriented?
	  c. Has the employee been through counseling or coaching sessions?
	
	2. Does the employee understand the expectations and job standards?
	
	3. Has the employee made promises to improve and not kept these promises?
	
	4. Is the individual's performance disrupting the team's performance or affecting business results?

DISCIPLINARY ACTION— THE LAST ALTERNATIVE

If you have tried your best as a manager to help an employee improve his/her performance and your efforts have not helped, you will need to initiate disciplinary action. This section will help you carry out that action.

DEFINITION

Disciplinary Action: A formal management system designed to get the employee to accept responsibility for his/her own behavior and agree to improve performance or face specific prescribed alternatives.

ROLE OF HUMAN RESOURCES OR PERSONNEL

Make sure you are working within your organization's policies when instituting a disciplinary action process. Check with your Human Resources or Personnel Manager *before* you move into the *"Steps in Disciplinary Action"* shown on the facing page.

DOCUMENTATION

The manager needs to keep an informal file on each employee which records dates and times of the counseling or coaching sessions. The manager's notes should include what was discussed, what was agreed upon and whether or not performance problems have improved, stayed the same or deteriorated. Specific and measurable performance objectives, should be defined in any disciplinary action plan. For a termination resulting from poor performance to occur, the manager should have a minimum of six counseling sessions recorded over a minimum period of six weeks.

ROLE OF YOUR MANAGER

Make sure your judgements and decisions will be supported by your manager. It is wise to keep him/her informed during the disciplinary action process. It is also a good idea to solicit his/her advice and approval.

REQUIRED STEPS IN DISCIPLINARY ACTION

LEVEL 1: VERBAL WARNING

A verbal warning is a conversation between an employee and manager to correct a performance problem by bringing it to the attention of the employee in a formal manner. The manager may wish to prepare a memo of the oral warning for his files after meeting with the employee. If such a memo is prepared a copy should be given to the employee. Verbal warnings are best given in private.

LEVEL 2: WRITTEN REMINDER

If the employee fails to make the desired performance changes following a verbal warning, a level 2 action should be taken. A *written reminder* is documentation of a formal discussion between a manager and an employee regarding a performance problem. The discussion is followed by a letter written to the employee which summarizes the conversation. A copy of this letter is generally sent to personnel and put in the employee's file.

LEVEL 3: TERMINATION DISCUSSION

Manager informs the employee that he/she is terminated from the company giving specific reasons which relate to the level 2 written reminder. The manager, in conjunction with the Personnel Department, is responsible for all termination and severance arrangements.

MORE INFORMATION ON TERMINATION

In order to avoid a wrongful discharge suit against the company, a manager should follow the Disciplinary Action Steps listed on page 49. However, a manager may consider the immediate suspension of the employee in these situations.*

1. Theft of company property

2. Absence from work for long periods of time

3. Assault on company property

4. Falsification of records or time cards

5. Criminal behavior

6. Insubordination

*(check your company policy on these situations before taking action)

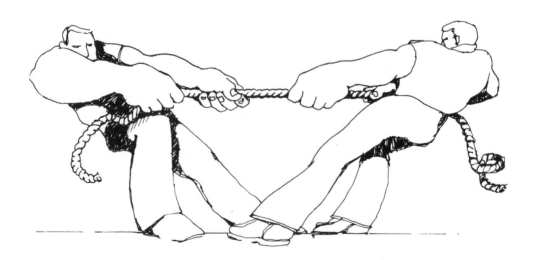

TERMINATION DECISIONS ARE RARELY SIMPLE OR EASY

SECTION: V
PULLING IT ALL TOGETHER

Case Studies For Coaching and Counseling

Develop a coaching and/or counseling plan for each of the following situations and compare your ideas with those of the author on the following page. Include in your plan the type of feedback you will use to motivate the employee.

CASE 1: You have just hired Tara. She is a software engineer who has just graduated from a major university. Although she is a recent graduate, you feel confident that she will bring enthusiasm and fresh ideas to her new job as a programmer. You have given her an important new project to work on.

You would: COACH _____   COUNSEL _____

(Please explain your answer):

_____

_____

_____

_____

_____

_____

_____

_____

_____

(Author's answer on page 57)

CASE 2:

Marsha is a Sales Manager in your retail firm. She has been with the company five years and seems to love her job. She was promoted last month to Sales Manager due to her ability to get along well with coworkers, customers and management. You have been swamped and have not had much time to spend with her. She just stopped by to discuss how she feels about her new job. She has stated that she is feeling overwhelmed by all the responsibilities and is unsure of her ability to handle all the pressure.

You would: COACH _____   COUNSEL _____

(Please explain your answer)

_____

_____

_____

_____

_____

_____

_____

_____

_____

(Author's answer of page 57)

CASE 3:

> Your boss of the last three years, Fred, stopped by for a chat. He has seemed ''out of sorts'' lately—depressed and irritable. You genuinely like working for Fred and feel he is an excellent role model for you as a manager. You don't know much about his personal life except that he is a family man and his wife, Mary, is Vice President of a large insurance company. Fred has three kids aged six, eight and ten. Fred is now saying that his wife has been offered a job in charge of a new division in Chicago and she really wants to take it. He is very concerned about the problems of relocating. He doesn't want to take the kids out of school. Also, he is a candidate for a promotion. He is having a difficult time trying to decide what to do. Fred asks for your advice.

You would: COACH _____   COUNSEL _____

(Please explain your answer)

_____

_____

_____

_____

_____

_____

_____

_____

_____

(Anthor's answer on page 57)

CASE 4:

Joan, your Production Control Supervisor, has been working for you for three years. She has been your star performer. She has implemented a new PC system, organized the work flow procedures and gets along well with all of the group managers. Unfortunately, a recent downturn in company sales has led to a budget freeze. Although you have an open manager's position, you are currently unable to promote Joan, even though she is your first choice. You know that Joan has a strong future with your company and want her to stay and "weather the current financial crisis." She has called you to set up an appointment to discuss her career options.

You would: COACH _____   COUNSEL _____

(Please explain your answer)

_____

_____

_____

_____

_____

_____

_____

_____

_____

(Author's answer on page 58)

CASE 5:

> Ned is a Marketing Specialist who is quite ambitious. He's been working for you for three months and you are basically pleased with the work he's done, although you have seen him overstep his boundaries at department meetings. You have had complaints from other team members about how he forces his ideas on others and seldom listens to theirs. He also seems to talk about *his* needs, career goals and strengths constantly. On two occasions you noticed he took credit for the ideas of other team members in front of upper management.

You would: COACH _____   COUNSEL _____

(Please explain your answer)

_____

_____

_____

_____

_____

_____

_____

_____

(Author's answer on page 58)

CASE 6: John has worked for you for the past year. He has been a steady, moderate performer, but lately you have become very concerned about his work. For the past six months you have noticed him coming in late, taking long lunches and leaving early. You have discussed your concerns with him and coached him on the importance of good work habits. He confided in you that he was having marital problems and his wife was seeking a separation. You gave him two weeks to "sort things out" but told him you expected him to be punctual and get back on track by then. Four weeks have gone by and his performance has continued to deteriorate. He has become belligerent and hostile and other members of the team have complained about his behavior. One mentioned that John has been drinking excessively every day at lunch.

You would: COACH _____   COUNSEL _____

(Please explain your answer)

_____

_____

_____

_____

_____

_____

_____

_____

(Author's answers on page 58)

AUTHOR'S SUGGESTED ANSWERS TO CASES

CASE 1 (page 51)

Answer: **This new employee needs to be coached.** Your coaching plan should include: 1) an orientation to the company, the team and the unit; 2) an initial work plan with realistic goals for the first few months; 3) training on any skills she needs for the job but does not possess; 4) communication of job standards, procedures, goals and rules within the team; 5) consistent supportive feedback in the form of advice and communicative reinforcement of recognizing desired performance.

CASE 2 (page 52)

Answer: **Both counseling and coaching are in order.** Your plan should include: 1) showing Marsha your support and reassurance by listening to her feelings and empathizing with her; 2) sending Marsha to management training class as you cannot assume that she knows how to manage simply because she now has a management title. Being a sales representative is quite different from being a sales manager; 3) coaching Marsha on how to make the transition from being an individual contributor to being a manager.

CASE 3 (page 53)

Answer: **Counseling is in order here,** as the boss has initiated the discussion and it does not involve a performance problem. Your counseling plan should include: 1) empathetic listening; 2) exploration of his feelings and concerns; 3) discussion of all possible alternatives and the consequences of each; 4) letting him know that you believe he can make the best decisions and offering him your continual support during this process.

AUTHOR'S SUGGESTED ANSWER
TO CASES (Continued)

CASE 4 (page 54)

Answer: **Counseling is the best choice.** Your counseling plan should include: 1) helping Joan explore her interests, values and goals; 2) assisting Joan in matching present opportunities in the company (perhaps you can help her transfer to an area with more mobility); 3) working with Joan to restructure her present job so that she is more challenged; 4) giving Joan opportunities for professional development in her present job, (i.e. attending classes or conferences, serving on a special task force, giving presentations to upper management).

CASE 5 (page 55)

Answer: **Coaching is the best choice.** Your coaching plan should include: 1) letting Ned know your expectations in terms of the need for him to build strong relationships with other team members; 2) communicating to him that you will reward collaborative and cooperative behavior, not competitive behavior; 3) determining his career goals and giving him advice about how to achieve his goals; (i.e. tying desired performance to his future career goals. Explain to him the need for interdependence with other people in order to get ahead in the unit and company); 4) reinforcing collaborative and cooperative behavior when he demonstrates it.

CASE 6 (page 56)

Answer: **Counseling and a disciplinary action plan are in order.** Your counseling plan should consist of the following: 1) informing John that you are very concerned about his job performance; 2) asking him to discuss the obstacles to his job performance; 3) describing the impact his performance has on you and the unit; 4) helping him explore alternative solutions to the performance problems; 5) getting a commitment from him to improve performance *immediately*; 6) scheduling a follow-up meeting and giving him reinforcement for performance improvement. If performance does not improve and remain consistent, 7) immediately have a Level I disciplinary discussion with him and document all your discussions. Also, inform your manager and check your personnel policy.

PERSONAL ACTION PLAN

Research has shown that if you use a new skill or knowledge right away you are likely to retain the knowledge or skill. Conversely, if you don't use it, you're likely to forget it. It helps to make a commitment to using new knowledge and skills in your professional and personal life.

Think about the information in this book. Review the exercises, questionnaires and case studies. What did you learn about yourself as a counselor? As a coach? Where do you need to improve? Then, develop your personal action plan below:

1. My counseling skills are effective in these areas:

2. My counseling skills need improvement in these areas:

3. My coaching skills are effective in these areas:

4. My coaching skills need improvement in these areas:

5. I will use my improved coaching and counseling skills with the following people on the following dates:

Person _____ Date _____

Person _____ Date _____

Your signature _____ Date: _____

NOTES

ABOUT THE FIFTY-MINUTE SERIES

We hope you enjoyed this book and found it valuable. If so, we have good news for you. This title is part of the best selling *FIFTY-MINUTE Series* of books. All other books are similar in size and identical in price. Several books are supported with a training video. These are identified by the symbol **V** next to the title.

Since the first *FIFTY-MINUTE* book appeared in 1986, more than five million copies have been sold worldwide. Each book was developed with the reader in mind. The result is a concise, high quality module written in a positive, readable self-study format.

FIFTY-MINUTE Books and Videos are available from your distributor or from Crisp Publications, Inc., 95 First Street, Los Altos, CA 94022. A free current catalog is available on request.

The complete list of *FIFTY-MINUTE Series* Books and Videos are listed on the following pages and organized by general subject area.

MANAGEMENT TRAINING (Cont.)

PERSONNEL/HUMAN RESOURCES

COMMUNICATIONS

CUSTOMER SERVICE/SALES TRAINING (CONT.)

SMALL BUSINESS/FINANCIAL PLANNING

ADULT LITERACY/BASIC LEARNING

CAREER BUILDING

To order books/videos from the FIFTY-MINUTE Series, please:

1. **CONTACT YOUR DISTRIBUTOR**

   or

2. **Write to Crisp Publications, Inc.**
   95 First Street   (415) 949-4888 - phone
   Los Altos, CA 94022   (415) 949-1610 - FAX